Kirstenbosch Gardening Series



# Bulbs

## A GUIDE TO THE SPECIES, CULTIVATION AND PROPAGATION OF SOUTH AFRICAN BULBS

Text and photographs by Graham Duncan
Line drawings by Jeanette Loedolff

Right: *Ornithogalum thyrsoides*

Below: *Watsonia borbonica* subsp. *ardernei* at Kirstenbosch in spring

Opposite: *Moraea villosa* subsp. *elandsmontana*

# CONTENTS

Left: *Sparaxis grandiflora* subsp. *acutiloba*

Right: *Strumaria barbariae*

Below: *Geissorhiza radians*

# INTRODUCTION

South Africa, in particular the winter rainfall region of the Western Cape, possesses one of the richest centres of bulbous plants in the world, with over 1 100 species, many of which have contributed handsomely to the international world of horticulture. During the early part of the seventeenth century, South African bulbs found their way to England and Europe where many were hybridized and 'improved', which resulted in the modern strains of common garden plants like *Gladiolus, Sparaxis, Freesia, Nerine* and *Agapanthus*, to mention just a few. While these hybridized strains have their place in modern horticulture, many of the wild bulbous species from South Africa are eminently suited to cultivation.

The popular term 'bulbous' refers to plants of a geophytic (growing from underground buds on specialized stems) nature, and include true bulbs (eg galtonias, lachenalias), corms (eg gladioli, watsonias), tuberous rootstocks (eg bulbines, zantedeschias) and rhizomatous rootstocks (eg clivias, kniphofias).

The South African bulbous flora can be conveniently placed into three groups, ie winter-growing, summer-growing and evergreen species.

It should be borne in mind that a number of genera require rather

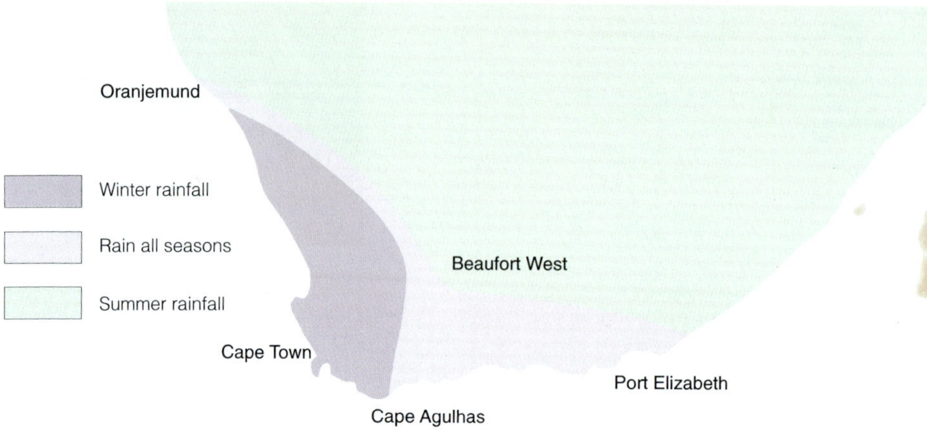


specialized cultivation techniques (eg *Cyrtanthus)* but the information in this publication is aimed at providing a general guide to the cultivation of our indigenous bulbous plants. For a more detailed exposition, the reader is referred to *Bulbous Plants of Southern Africa: a guide to their cultivation and propagation*, by N.M. du Plessis and G.D. Duncan, with watercolours by Elise Bodley (see further reading list).

For the purposes of this publication, bulbous species belonging to twelve different families are covered – Agapanthaceae, Alliaceae (alliums), Amaryllidaceae, Araceae (arums), Asphodelaceae (eg bulbinellas), Colchicaceae (eg *Gloriosa*, Haemodoraceae (eg *Wachendorfia*), Hyacinthaceae (eg lachenalias), Hypoxidaceae, Iridaceae, Oxalidaceae and Tecophilaeaceae (cyanellas).

Bulbous members of the families Orchidaceae and Geraniaceae (pelargoniums) are not covered in this publication as their cultivation requirements are somewhat different.

**The family Agapanthaceae**

*Agapanthus* is the only genus belonging to this family and it is endemic in southern Africa, where its wide distribution extends

Left: *Tulbaghia simmleri* – Family Alliaceae

Opposite: *Agapanthus inapertus* subsp. *pendulus* 'Graskop' – Family Agapanthaceae

from the Cape Peninsula in the Western Cape to the mountain ranges just south of the Limpopo River in the Northern Province. *Agapanthus* was formerly placed under the family Alliaceae. This extremely variable genus consists of ten species and can conveniently be divided into two major groups of evergreen and deciduous species. The evergreen members occur in the winter rainfall and year-round rainfall regions, while the deciduous species occur in the summer rainfall regions, and are dormant during the cold dry winters. *Agapanthus* ranks among the most easily cultivated bulbous plants in mild climates. They are ideal garden and container plants, and also make excellent cutflowers.

**The family Alliaceae**

The Alliaceae, formerly a part of the Liliaceae, is a widely distributed family of which the mainly Northern Hemisphere genus *Allium* is the most important. The major centres of distribution for the whole family are Mediterranean Europe, Asia, North and South America and southern Africa. The southern African genera comprise *Tulbaghia* and a single species of *Allium*. The horticulturally important genus *Tulbaghia* consists of about twenty species and is noted for the strong onion or garlic smell given off by the injured parts of most species. There are both evergreen and deciduous tulbaghias, most of which are extremely easy to cultivate. The evergreen species are particularly useful as groundcovers and as container plants in mild climates.

**The family Amaryllidaceae**

The amaryllids form a very large group of over sixty genera and are concentrated mainly in southern Africa, with smaller centres in Andean South

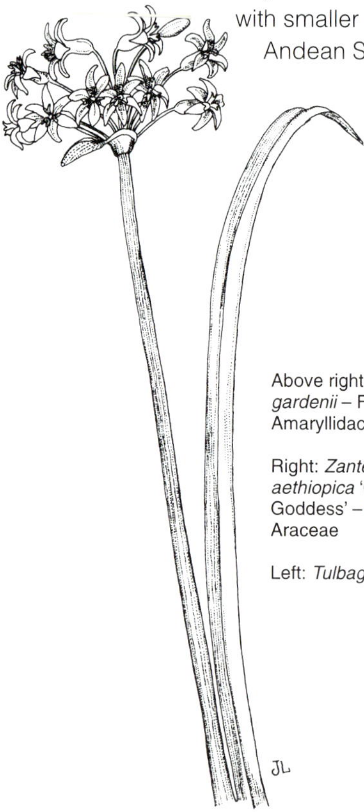

Above right: *Clivia gardenii* – Family Amaryllidaceae

Right: *Zantedeschia aethiopica* 'Green Goddess' – Family Araceae

Left: *Tulbaghia simmleri*

the most horticulturally important genera found in southern Africa include *Amaryllis, Clivia, Crinum, Cyrtanthus, Nerine* and *Scadoxus. Hippeastrum* is a large American genus occurring from the West Indies and Mexico to Argentina, from which the large and colourful hybrids of today originate. Other important Northern Hemisphere members include *Narcissus* and *Leucojum*. Most of the southern African amaryllids are deciduous and hysteranthous, ie their new leaves are produced after the flowers have finished.

**The family Araceae**

This very large family is distributed worldwide, but occurs predominantly in the warmer regions. The South American genus *Caladium* and the Asian genus *Alocasia* are grown for their decorative foliage, and several species of the European and Mediterranean genus *Arum* are cultivated for their curious spathes and spotted or glossy leaves. *Zantedeschia* is endemic to southern Africa and is the only important ornamental member from this region. This mainly summer-growing genus is cultivated worldwide both for its excellent cutflowers and as a container plant, and numerous colourful hybrids have been raised in New Zealand, where it is an important horticultural crop.

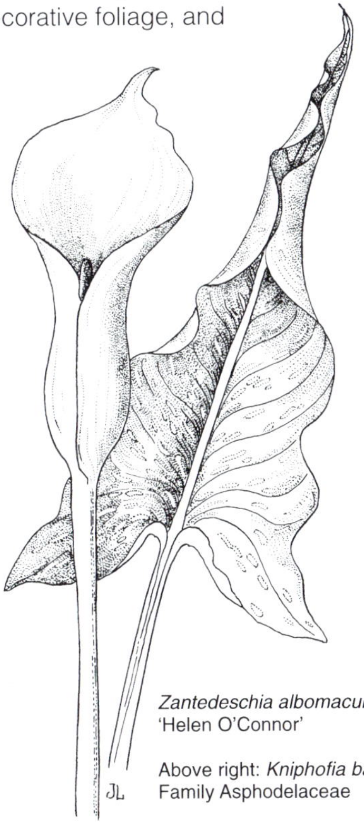

*Zantedeschia albomaculata* 'Helen O'Connor'

Above right: *Kniphofia baurii* – Family Asphodelaceae

**The family Asphodelaceae**

The Asphodelaceae (formerly a part of the Liliaceae) comprise approximately seventeen genera and are widely distributed in the Old World, concentrated mainly in southern Africa. *Bulbine, Bulbinella, Kniphofia* and *Trachyandra* are the most important geophytic members in

Left: *Gloriosa superba* – Family Colchicaceae

Opposite above: *Veltheimia capensis* – Family Hyacinthaceae

Opposite below: *Wachendorfia brachyandra* – Family Haemodoraceae

Below: *Gloriosa superba*

southern Africa, of which *Bulbinella* and *Kniphofia* are horticulturally the most noteworthy. Several important succulent members such as *Gasteria, Aloe* and *Haworthia* also occur in this region. The genus *Kniphofia* is reasonably hardy and is particularly widely grown in the United Kingdom, where countless striking hybrids have been raised.

**The family Colchicaceae**

The distribution of this family (formerly a part of the Liliaceae) ranges through both the summer and winter rainfall areas of South Africa, and extends through Africa to the Mediterranean and western Asia, where *Colchicum*, the largest genus, is found. Horticulturally the most important South African genera include *Gloriosa*, *Littonia*, *Sandersonia* and *Onixotis*, all of which are deciduous. The monotypic *Sandersonia aurantiaca* has been very successfully commercialized in New Zealand, where it is widely grown for the export cutflower trade due to its excellent vase-life.

### The family Haemodoraceae

The Haemodoraceae are found mainly in the Southern Hemisphere; their distribution is centred in Australia with smaller centres

Alice Notten

in South Africa and South to North America. *Dilatris* and *Wachendorfia* are the two most important genera from South Africa, where both are endemic to the winter rainfall region. The stately *Wachendorfia thyrsiflora* is the only evergreen species in this genus and it is also the most widely grown, due to its bold yellow spikes and preference for poorly drained, boggy conditions. The well-known genus *Anigozanthos* or 'Kangaroo Paw' is the most commonly grown representative from Australia. The rootstocks of all members of this family are a characteristic reddish-orange colour.

### The family Hyacinthaceae

Members of this family (formerly a part of the Liliaceae) are particularly well represented in southern Africa and in the

region from the Mediterranean to southwestern Asia. Noteworthy genera from the Northern Hemisphere include *Hyacinthus* and *Muscari*, and several genera have a very wide distribution and occur in both southern Africa and in Europe or Asia, such as *Ornithogalum*, *Scilla, Urginea* and *Dipcadi*. The most horticulturally important genera from South Africa are *Eucomis*, *Galtonia, Lachenalia, Ornithogalum* and *Veltheimia*. Several less well known, monotypic genera also occur here, such as *Amphisiphon*, *Daubenya* and *Whiteheadia*.

**The family Hypoxidaceae**

This family is found mainly in the Southern Hemisphere and especially in southern Africa, Australia and South America. The large genus *Hypoxis* is very well represented in southern Africa, and also occurs in southern Asia, Australia and South America. The rootstock of *Hypoxis hemerocallidea* has been used medicinally

for generations by some of the indigenous peoples of South Africa, and recent medical research has revealed that its properties increase the body's natural resistance to disease. The most important ornamental genus from South Africa is *Rhodohypoxis*, which is completely hardy and widely grown as a container plant in the Northern Hemisphere.

### The family Iridaceae

This large and extremely diverse family consists of more than sixty genera and has a worldwide distribution. The region of greatest genus and species concentration is Africa south of the equator, and the winter rainfall area of South Africa in particular. It is the genera belonging to this family which have made South Africa's greatest contribution to world horticulture, most notably *Gladiolus*, *Freesia, Crocosmia, Dierama, Ixia, Sparaxis, Tritonia* and *Babiana*. Most important among these is undoubtedly *Gladiolus*, which has been bred overseas to such an extent that today's rather oversized cultivars bear scant resemblance to their more modest, visually pleasing ancestors. The large genus *Iris* is confined to the Northern Hemisphere where it occurs over a very wide range of habitats.

Opposite above: *Rhodohypoxis baurii* – Family Hypoxidaceae

Left: *Geissorhiza tulbaghensis* – Family Iridaceae

Above: *Oxalis purpurea* – Family Oxalidaceae

### The family Oxalidaceae

The Oxalidaceae comprises seven genera of which only *Oxalis* and *Biophytum* occur in southern Africa. The very large genus *Oxalis* consists of about eight hundred species and is distributed worldwide; most of these occur in South America, and there are about two hundred species in South Africa. Our best known *Oxalis*, the exceptionally prolific *Oxalis pes-caprae*, has become naturalized in temperate regions around the world, and in Australia it is a declared noxious weed. Similarly, there

have been several weedy introductions to South Africa, of which the worst is probably the 'Creeping Sorrel', *Oxalis corniculata* from North America.

**The family Tecophilaeaceae**

Members of the Tecophilaeaceae occur mainly in the Southern Hemisphere and are concentrated in South America and South Africa. *Cyanella* is the only horticulturally noteworthy genus from South Africa, and it is an exclusively winter-growing, summer-dormant geophyte with a deep-seated corm. The corms of several *Cyanella* species are known to be eaten by some of the indigenous peoples of southern Africa. *Cyanella hyacinthoides* and *C. orchidiformis* seed themselves prolifically under cultivation and can become invasive if not kept in check. The beautiful genus *Tecophilaea* consists of two species which occur in Chile, and are highly prized as container subjects.

Opposite: *Cyanella alba* – Family Tecophilaeaceae

Below: *Gladiolus carmineus*

Right: *Nerine sarniensis* (dark pink form)

Below right: *Watsonia humilis*

# CULTIVATION OF WINTER-GROWING SPECIES

The species belonging to this group occur naturally in the Richtersveld, throughout Namaqualand, the Western, south-western and southern Cape and the Little Karoo. The Great Karoo contains fewer species and the diversity decreases markedly as one moves eastwards, terminating in the Eastern Cape. The winter-growing species can be grown outdoors successfully in most parts of the country except the very

coldest areas and those areas which have very wet summers. The growth cycle of most species in this group is characterized by the production of new vegetative growth in autumn, as soon as temperatures begin to fall after the long, dry summer. This is followed by very rapid vegetative growth during winter, and by flowering in spring. Seed production and dispersal follows in early summer, and the plant becomes dormant until the following autumn. The growth cycle of most members of the Amaryllidaceae is somewhat different in that flowering takes place in late summer, before vegetative growth begins. There is also a small group of species that flower at the end of the growing season. In general, the vast majority of the deciduous, winter-growing species are not hardy in very cold climates, but certain species like *Gladiolus tristis* are known to be fairly hardy when

Top: *Gethyllis linearis*

Above: *Moraea neopavonia*

Opposite above: *Amaryllis belladonna* (white form)

Opposite below: *Lachenalia orthopetala*

Left: *Bulbinella nutans*

Opposite: *Moraea tricolor*

Left: *Strumaria tenella* flowering *en masse* on a granite outcrop at Langebaan

Below: *Moraea herrei* *(Barnardiella spiralis)*

grown outdoors in mild parts of the Northern Hemisphere, such as in the southwest of England. Cold tender species require the protection of the cool greenhouse.

**Container subjects**

With the obvious exception of the more robust members of this group, such as the larger watsonias, the vast majority of these species can be very successfully cultivated in containers. In many instances, container cultivation is the only practical manner in which to grow many of the more delicate species of *Gethyllis*, *Gladiolus* and *Ixia*, for example.

Aspect

In general, a sunny aspect with free air circulation is required for the winter-growing species. In areas with mild winters, pots can be arranged

together in groups on a veranda or patio, and flat-dwellers can use window-boxes on a sunny balcony. It is important that pots should not be placed in positions where they will overheat on very hot days. In areas with heavy winter rainfall, such as in the southern suburbs of the Cape Peninsula, the more delicate species are best grown under cover. The avid grower of

*Babiana ringens*

Opposite above: *Boophone haemanthoides*

Opposite below: *Watsonia hysterantha* flowering in cracks of granite outcrops above Saldanha Bay

such bulbous plants will be inclined to erect a structure with benches, open sides and glass-fibre roof, where an ever-expanding collection can be maintained.

### Growing medium

Good drainage of the growing medium is one of the most important factors when cultivating bulbous plants. In the wild, the vast majority of winter-growing species occur in nutrient-poor soils which drain rapidly – the temptation to grow these species in rich, water-retentive media must thus be avoided.

The most important component of the growing medium is sand, which should preferably be a medium-grained, washed river-sand, available from most retail nurseries. For easily cultivated species such as *Gladiolus carneus, Lachenalia unicolor* and *Moraea loubseri*, a medium consisting of two parts river- or industrial sand, one part loam and one part fine compost is recommended. For less easily cultivated species such as *Hessea breviflora*, *Gladiolus trichonemifolius* and *Lachenalia ameliae*, the amount of loam should be reduced considerably, or dispensed with entirely. Difficult species such as *Tritonia watermeyeri*, *Gladiolus debilis*, *Ixia viridiflora*, and the amaryllid genera such as *Gethyllis*, *Haemanthus* and *Strumaria*, should be grown in a medium of

Left: *Cyrtanthus staadensis*

Below: *Ornithogalum dubium* (reddish-orange form)

Opposite: *Ornithogalum dubium* (orange form)

three parts river- or industrial sand and one part fine compost, or the compost can be dispensed with entirely, in which case a mixture of equal parts river- and industrial sand is recommended. Growers will discover their own ideal growing medium – but there can be no doubt that the more sand incorporated into the growing medium, the better the results will be.

A layer of broken crocks, or stone or bark chips should always be placed over the drainage holes at the bottom of the container, and a thin layer of fine compost should be placed over this to prevent the finer growing medium from washing out. The rest of the container is then filled with the appropriate growing medium.

Ordinary deep, brown plastic pots are ideal – a 15 cm pot is suited to the low-growing genera such as *Oxalis* and *Polyxena*, while a 20 cm pot is suitable for medium-sized species of *Geissorhiza*, *Lachenalia* and *Romulea*. Taller species of *Gladiolus*, *Ixia*, and all the dwarf amaryllid genera such as *Gethyllis*, *Hessea* and the smaller nerines require a 25 cm pot.

A 30 cm pot is recommended for those species with vigorous root systems such as *Moraea aristata* and the dwarf watsonias.

A 35 cm pot is recommended for those species with very large bulbs, such as *Brunsvigia orientalis*, *Boophone haemanthoides* and *Veltheimia capensis*.

### Planting

Rootstocks are planted out from March to May, April being the most suitable month. Members of the family Amaryllidaceae, all of which have perennial fleshy roots, should not be disturbed once they have established, but if they have to be transplanted, it should be done immediately after the new leaves start to appear, while the bulbs are in active growth.

The depth of planting depends on the species but, as a general rule, this should

Above: *Moraea gigandra*

Left: *Hesperantha pauciflora*

Opposite: *Onixotis stricta*

### Recommended winter-growing species for containers

| Species | Common name | Species | Common name |
|---|---|---|---|
| Amaryllidaceae | | Colchicaceae | |
| *Boophone haemanthoides* | kwaslelie | *Onixotis stricta* | vleiblommetjie |
| *Brunsvigia bosmaniae* | maartblom | | |
| *Brunsvigia gregaria* | | Hyacinthaceae | |
| *Brunsvigia marginata* | | *Daubenya aurea* | |
| *Brunsvigia minor* | seeroogblom | *Lachenalia aloides* | klipbelletjie |
| *Cybistetes longifolia* | malgaslelie | *Lachenalia arbuthnotiae* | |
| *Gethyllis afra* | koekoemakranka | *Lachenalia bulbifera* | rooinaeltjie |
| *Gethyllis britteniana* | | *Lachenalia fistulosa* | |
| *Gethyllis ciliaris* | | *Lachenalia hirta* | |
| *Gethyllis linearis* | | *Lachenalia mathewsii* | |
| *Gethyllis verticillata* | fraaikoekoe-makranka | *Lachenalia mutabilis* | bontviooltjie |
| | | *Lachenalia namaquensis* | |
| *Gethyllis villosa* | skurwekoekoe-makranka | *Lachenalia orchioides* | groenviooltjie |
| | | *Lachenalia orthopetala* | |
| *Haemanthus coccineus* | velskoenblaar, April fool | *Lachenalia pustulata* | knoppiesviooltjie |
| | | *Lachenalia rubida* | sandkalossie |
| *Haemanthus crispus* | | *Lachenalia thomasiae* | |
| *Haemanthus pubescens* | poeierkwas | *Lachenalia trichophylla* | |
| *Hessea breviflora* | | *Lachenalia unicolor* | persviooltjie |
| *Hessea tenella* | | *Lachenalia viridiflora* | |
| *Nerine humilis* | berglelie | *Ornithogalum dubium* | geeltjienkerintjee |
| *Nerine sarniensis* | Guernsey lily | *Ornithogalum maculatum* | slangblom |
| *Strumaria barbariae* | | *Ornithogalum thyrsoides* | chinkerinchee |
| *Strumaria salteri* | | *Veltheimia capensis* | sandlelie |
| *Strumaria truncata* | Namaqualand snowdrop | | |
| | | Iridaceae | |
| *Strumaria unguiculata* | | *Babiana augustifolia* | vleibobbejaantjie |
| | | *Babiana blanda* | |
| Asphodelaceae | | *Babiana disticha* | bobbejaantjie |
| *Bulbinella cauda-felis* | katstert | *Babiana nana* | klipuintjie |
| *Bulbinella latifolia* | | *Babiana pygmaea* | geelbobbejaantjie |
| var. *doleritica* | swartturk | *Babiana ringens* | rotstert |
| *Bulbinella nutans* | | *Babiana rubrocyanea* | rooiblou-bobbejaantjie |
| var. *nutans* | seeroogkatstert | | |
| | | *Babiana stricta* | bobbejaantjie |
| | | *Babiana villosa* | rooibobbejaantjie |
| | | *Ferraria densepunctulata* | grysuiltjie |
| | | *Freesia alba* | ruikpypie |

be at a depth of about three times the height of the rootstock. Exceptions to this rule are the androcymbiums, babianas and cyanellas, which are planted twice as deep, while the bulbines, bulbinellas, dwarf ornithogalums and most amaryllids are planted just below the surface. *Veltheimia capensis* and some of the boophones are planted with at least two thirds of the bulb above ground level.

### Watering

Once planted, pots should be watered well, and then not again until the leaf

| Species | Common name |
|---|---|
| *Freesia corymbosa* | kammetjie |
| *Freesia fergusoniae* | Riversdale freesia |
| *Geissorhiza darlingensis* | geelkelkiewyn |
| *Geissorhiza inflexa* | |
| *Geissorhiza mathewsii* | |
| *Geissorhiza monanthos* | bleeksysie |
| *Geissorhiza radians* | wynblommetjie, witringkelkiewyn |
| *Geissorhiza splendidissima* | blue pride-of-Nieuwoudtville |
| *Geissorhiza tulbaghensis* | |
| *Gladiolus alatus* | kalkoentjie |
| *Gladiolus carinatus* | blue Afrikander |
| *Gladiolus carmineus* | cliff gladiolus |
| *Gladiolus carneus* | painted lady |
| *Gladiolus debilis* | painted lady |
| *Gladiolus equitans* | rooikalkoentjie |
| *Gladiolus floribundus* | |
| *Gladiolus gracilis* | bloupypie |
| *Gladiolus huttonii* | |
| *Gladiolus liliaceus* | kaneelaandblom |
| *Gladiolus maculatus* | aandblom |
| *Gladiolus orchidiflorus* | groenkalkoentjie |
| *Gladiolus priorii* | rooi Afrikaner |
| *Gladiolus stefaniae* | |
| *Gladiolus trichonemifolius* | botterlelie |
| *Gladiolus tristis* | vlei aandblom |
| *Hesperantha pauciflora* | pink hesperantha |
| *Hesperantha vaginata* | harlequin hesperantha |
| *Ixia campanulata* | |
| *Ixia curta* | bruinoogkalossie |
| *Ixia framesii* | rooikalossie |
| *Ixia frederickii* | |
| *Ixia leipoldtii* | |
| *Ixia lutea* | bleekkalossie |
| *Ixia maculata* | geelkalossie |
| *Ixia scillaris* | agretjie |
| *Ixia viridiflora* | green ixia |

| Species | Common name |
|---|---|
| *Moraea aristata* | blou ooguintjie |
| *Moraea atropunctata* | |
| *Moraea barnardiella* | |
| *Moraea comptonii* | |
| *Moraea elegans* | poublom |
| *Moraea gigandra* | |
| *Moraea insolens* | |
| *Moraea loubseri* | |
| *Moraea neopavonia* | peacock flower |
| *Moraea ovalifolia* | oorlosieblom |
| *Moraea tricolor* | spoguintjie |
| *Moraea versicolor* | |
| *Moraea villosa* | uiltjie |
| *Romulea flava* | geelfrutang |
| *Romulea monadelpha* | karoosatynblom |
| *Romulea obscura* | kolfrutang |
| *Romulea rosea* | frutang |
| *Romulea sabulosa* | satynblom |
| *Romulea subfistulosa* | |
| *Sparaxis elegans* | spogfluweeltjie |
| *Sparaxis grandiflora* | botterblom |
| *Sparaxis tricolor* | fluweeltjie |
| *Tritonia crocata* | kalkoentjie |
| *Tritonia squalida* | kalkoentjie |
| *Tritonia watermeyeri* | |
| *Watsonia aletroides* | rooikanolpypie |
| *Watsonia coccinea* | rooipypie |
| *Watsonia humilis* | waspypie |
| *Watsonia laccata* | |
| *Watsonia spectabilis* | |
| *Watsonia stenosiphon* | |
| **Oxalidaceae** | |
| *Oxalis hirta* | |
| *Oxalis obtusa* | suring |
| *Oxalis pardalis* | |
| *Oxalis purpurea* | |
| *Oxalis versicolor* | |

*Romulea monadelpha*

shoots begin to appear, after which a good soaking every fortnight is recommended for most species, as opposed to light applications at irregular intervals. Over-watering of container-grown species will soon lead to rotting, and as a general rule it is preferable for the growing medium to be

slightly dry rather than too wet. This applies particularly to members of the family Amaryllidaceae, such as *Gethyllis*, *Hessea* and *Strumaria*, which should be watered only once a month. Exceptions to the general rule are species of *Geissorhiza*, such as *G. darlingensis* and *G. radians*, as well as *Onixotis stricta*, which require a continually moist medium during the growing period.

Towards the end of spring, as temperatures rise, the plants begin to go dormant, which is indicated by a yellowing of the leaves. Watering must now be withheld completely, and as soon as seed has been harvested, and the foliage has

completely withered, the containers can be placed in a cool dry place and stored.

## Garden subjects

Relatively few species of winter-growing geophytes are suited to general garden cultivation because of their delicate nature, extremely short flowering period, the depredations of moles and porcupines, and their inability to withstand garden irrigation during the dormant period.

## Aspect and growing medium

As with container subjects, a sunny aspect with free air circulation is required for the winter-growers. Soil must be very well drained, but generally those species suited to garden culture are able to withstand less free draining soils than species that can only be grown in containers. Drainage can be improved by mixing in large quantities of fine compost and sand.

Slightly sloping ground is ideal for planting as it allows for good water run-off. The rockery is a suitable spot in which to

Left: *Romulea flava*

Below: *Strumaria truncata*

plant groups of the same species, but where moles are prevalent the smaller species will have to be grown in sunken wire baskets. Bulbous plants are displayed to great advantage by interplanting with low-growing spring annuals such as nemesias and Bokbaai vygies (*Dorotheanthus bellidiformis*).

## Planting

The rootstocks should be set out from March to May at the same depths recommended for container subjects, but in extremely sandy soil they can be planted deeper.

## Watering

After planting, the rootstocks should be watered well and not again until the leaf

*Ixia curta*

Above left: *Lachenalia aloides* var. *quadricolor*

Above right: *Ixia polystachya* var. *crassifolia*

*Babiana rubrocyanea*

## Recommended winter-growing species for gardens

| Species | Common name |
|---|---|
| Amaryllidaceae | |
| *Amaryllis belladonna* | March lily |
| *Brunsvigia bosmaniae* | maartblom |
| *Brunsvigia gregaria* | |
| *Brunsvigia josephinae* | kandelaarblom |
| *Brunsvigia orientalis* | candelabra flower |
| *Cybistetes longifolia* | malgaslelie |
| *Haemanthus coccineus* | velskoenblaar, April fool |
| *Haemanthus pubescens* | poeierkwas |
| *Haemanthus sanguineus* | April fool |
| *Nerine humilis* | berglelie |
| *Nerine sarniensis* | Guernsey lily |
| Araceae (arum lilies) | |
| *Zantedeschia aethiopica* | arum lily |
| Asphodelaceae | |
| *Bulbinella cauda-felis* | katstert |
| *Bulbinella nutans* | seeroogkatstert |
| Colchicaceae | |
| *Onixotis stricta* | vleiblommetjie |
| Haemodoraceae | |
| *Wachendorfia brachyandra* | bruinkanol |
| *Wachendorfia paniculata* | spinnekopblom |
| *Wachendorfia thyrsiflora* | rooikanol |
| Hyacinthaceae | |
| *Lachenalia aloides* | klipbelletjie |
| *Lachenalia arbuthnotiae* | |
| *Lachenalia bulbifera* | rooinaeltjie |
| *Lachenalia contaminata* | wild hyacinth |
| *Lachenalia mathewsii* | |
| *Lachenalia pustulata* | knoppiesviooltjie |
| *Lachenalia unicolor* | persviooltjie |
| *Ornithogalum thyrsoides* | chinkerinchee |
| Iridaceae | |
| *Babiana angustifolia* | vleibobbejaantjie |
| *Babiana disticha* | bobbejaantjie |
| *Babiana rubrocyanea* | rooibloubobbe-jaantjie |
| *Babiana stricta* | bobbejaantjie |
| *Babiana villosa* | rooibobbejaantjie |
| *Chasmanthe aethiopica* | suurkanol |
| *Chasmanthe bicolor* | |
| *Chasmanthe floribunda* | suurkanol |
| *Freesia alba* | |
| *Gladiolus carneus* | painted lady |
| *Gladiolus priorii* | rooi Afrikaner |
| *Gladiolus tristis* | vlei aandblom |
| *Gladiolus undulatus* | rooibontpypie |
| *Ixia flexuosa* | koringblommetjie |
| *Ixia lutea* | |
| *Ixia maculata* | geelkalossie |
| *Ixia polystachya* | witkalossie |
| *Ixia viridiflora* | green ixia |
| *Moraea aristata* | blou ooguintjie |
| *Moraea comptonii* | |
| *Moraea elegans* | poublom |
| *Moraea gigandra* | |
| *Moraea loubseri* | |
| *Moraea ochroleuca* | geeltulp |
| *Moraea villosa* | uiltjie |
| *Romulea flava* | geelfrutang |
| *Romulea monadelpha* | karoosatynblom |
| *Romulea sabulosa* | satynblom |
| *Sparaxis grandiflora* | botterblom |
| *Sparaxis tricolor* | fluweeltjie |
| *Tritonia crocata* | kalkoentjie |
| *Tritonia squalida* | kalkoentjie |
| *Watsonia borbonica* | |
| *Watsonia hysterantha* | herfskanolpypie |
| *Watsonia marginata* | kanolpypie |
| *Watsonia meriana* | lakpypie |
| *Watsonia vanderspuyiae* | |
| Oxalidaceae | |
| *Oxalis pardalis* | |
| *Oxalis purpurea* | |
| *Oxalis versicolor* | |
| Tecophilaeaceae | |
| *Cyanella alba* | toe-toe uintjie |
| *Cyanella lutea* | five fingers |

shoots appear. A fortnightly soaking should be given if natural precipitation is lacking. The species recommended for garden culture are generally those that can withstand a fair amount of garden irrigation during the dormant period, but if one is unable to lift, store and replant them every year, they are best placed in areas of the garden that receive as little water as possible during summer.

*Ixia lutea* var. *lutea*

Top: *Watsonia marginata* (white form)

Right: *Moraea elegans* (*Homeria elegans*)

Opposite: *Watsonia borbonica* subsp. *ardernei*

Opposite: *Crinum campanulatum*

Below: *Rhodohypoxis baurii* 'Douglas'

# CULTIVATION OF SUMMER-GROWING SPECIES

The summer-growing species occur naturally in the Northern Province, Mpumalanga, Gauteng, KwaZulu-Natal, Free State and the eastern part of the Northern Cape and the Eastern Cape. Their growth-cycle is generally characterized by the production of new vegetative growth in spring, followed by rapid growth in summer and flowering in midsummer to late autumn, and then by a dormant period in winter. Many members of the Amaryllidaceae are, however, characterized by flowering at the beginning of the growing season (eg *Boophone disticha*). The summer-growers can generally be grown outdoors throughout the country except in areas with very cold or excessively wet winters. Some species, like the summer-growing agapanthus and scillas, do however withstand very wet winters, provided the soil is well drained. Several species of deciduous, summer-growing bulbous plants are hardy in mild parts of the Northern Hemisphere, such as in the southwest of England. These include *Nerine bowdenii*, *Rhodohypoxis* species, *Crocosmia* species and *Galtonia candicans*. However, most of the deciduous summer-growers require the protection of the cool greenhouse in very cold climates.

grown under cover. This also applies to areas with winter rainfall, as the containers can easily be stored in a dry place during the winter dormant period.

### Growing medium

As with the winter-growing species, the most important component of the growing medium is a medium-grained, washed river- or industrial sand, used in varying proportions with fine compost, depending on the species. For easily cultivated

Left: *Ammocharis coranica*

Below: *Boophone disticha*

Opposite: *Sandersonia aurantiaca*

### Container subjects

Container cultivation is the only practical manner in which to grow many of the more delicate of our summer-growing *Cyrtanthus* and nerines, for example. In general, however, most summer-growing species are more suited to garden cultivation than to containers, due mainly to their rather robust nature.

### Aspect

A full sun or partially shaded position with free air circulation is required for most species. In areas with heavy summer rainfall, the more delicate species are best

### Recommended summer-growing species for containers

| Species | Common name | Species | Common name |
|---|---|---|---|
| Amaryllidaceae | | Colchicaceae | |
| *Ammocharis coranica* | Corana lily, gifbol | *Gloriosa superba* | flame lily |
| *Ammocharis nerinoides* | | *Littonia modesta* | geelklokkie |
| *Boophone disticha* | century plant | *Sandersonia aurantiaca* | Christmas bells |
| *Crinum lugardiae* | | | |
| *Crinum moorei* | Natal lily | Hyacinthaceae | |
| *Cyrtanthus breviflorus* | vuurlelie | *Galtonia viridiflora* | |
| *Cyrtanthus clavatus* | | *Lindneria clavata* | |
| *Cyrtanthus falcatus* | fire lily | | |
| *Cyrtanthus galpinii* | puruutjie | Hypoxidaceae | |
| *Cyrtanthus loddigesianus* | | *Rhodohypoxis baurii* | rooisterretjie |
| *Cyrtanthus smithiae* | | *Rhodohypoxis baurii* | |
| *Haemanthus humilis* | velskoenblaar | 'Douglas' | |
| *Haemanthus montanus* | | *Rhodohypoxis milloides* | |
| *Nerine bowdenii* | | *Rhodohypoxis rubella* | |
| *Nerine laticoma* | | | |
| *Nerine undulata* | | Iridaceae | |
| *Scadoxus multiflorus* | blood flower | *Gladiolus oppositiflorus* | |
| *Scadoxus puniceus* | snake lily | *Gladiolus saundersii* | |
| | | *Hesperantha huttonii* | |
| Araceae (arums) | | *Tritonia disticha* | |
| *Zantedeschia albomaculata* | kleinvarkblom | | |
| *Zantedeschia pentlandii* | yellow arum | | |
| *Zantedeschia rehmannii* | persvarkblom | | |

species such as *Cyrtanthus falcatus* and *Haemanthus montanus*, a medium consisting of two parts river- or industrial sand and one part fine compost is recommended. Less easily-cultivated species like *Cyrtanthus loddigesianus* and *Boophone disticha* should have a reduced proportion of compost, while difficult species such as *Cyrtanthus smithiae* and *Gladiolus cruentus* should be grown in a medium of equal parts river- and industrial sand. As with the winter-growing species, deep, brown plastic pots are ideal – a 20 cm pot is suitable for the smaller species of *Cyrtanthus* and *Nerine* while a 25 cm pot is suitable for larger members of these genera, as well as the dwarf *Eucomis* species. A 30 cm pot is needed for robust species such as *Nerine bowdenii*,

*Gladiolus saundersii* and *Tritonia disticha*, while a 35 cm pot is required for very large species such as *Boophone disticha* and *Scadoxus multiflorus*.

## Planting

The general rule of a depth of about three times the height of the rootstock applies to most members of the Iridaceae, whereas the Amaryllidaceae, Asphodelaceae and Hyacinthaceae are usually planted much nearer the surface, or with the necks protruding above ground level (eg *Cyrtanthus falcatus*). At least two thirds of the bulbs of *Boophone disticha* and *Lindneria clavata*, for example, are planted above ground level to prevent rotting.

The summer-growers are planted out in spring, but members of the Amaryllidaceae, once planted, should remain undisturbed for many years.

*Eucomis comosa*

Right: *Eucomis autumnalis*

Opposite: *Crinum moorei*

### Watering

A good soaking once a week is recommended for most of the summer-growers when grown in containers. Many of the *Cyrtanthus* require far less frequent watering, say once every three weeks for species such as *C. smithiae* and *C. clavatus*.

## Garden subjects

### Aspect and growing medium

The summer-growing species suitable for garden culture generally prefer a very rich, but well-drained soil, in a partially shaded or full sun position. Many of these species are not adversely affected by heavy winter rainfall during their dormant period and are thus relatively low maintenance plants,

**Recommended summer-growing species for gardens**

| Species | Common name | Species | Common name |
|---|---|---|---|
| Agapanthaceae | | Colchicaceae | |
| *Agapanthus campanulatus* | | *Gloriosa superba* | flame lily |
| *Agapanthus caulescens* | | *Littonia modesta* | geelklokkie |
| *Agapanthus coddii* | | | |
| *Agapanthus inapertus* | | Hyacinthaceae | |
| | | *Eucomis autumnalis* | pineapple flower |
| Amaryllidaceae | | *Eucomis bicolor* | |
| *Ammocharis coranica* | Corana lily, gifbol | *Eucomis comosa* | |
| *Brunsvigia natalensis* | kandelaarblom | *Eucomis pole-evansii* | |
| *Brunsvigia radulosa* | misryblom | *Galtonia candicans* | berg lily |
| *Crinum bulbispermum* | Orange River lily | *Galtonia viridiflora* | |
| *Crinum campanulatum* | vleilelie | | |
| *Crinum graminicola* | graslelie | Hypoxidaceae | |
| *Crinum macowanii* | boslelie | *Hypoxis hemerocallidea* | African potato, gifbol |
| *Crinum moorei* | Natal lily | | |
| *Cyrtanthus falcatus* | fire lily | | |
| *Nerine bowdenii* | | Iridaceae | |
| *Nerine krigei* | | *Crocosmia aurea* | |
| *Nerine undulata* | | *Crocosmia pottsii* | |
| *Scadoxus multiflorus* | blood flower | *Gladiolus dalenii* | sword lily |
| *Scadoxus puniceus* | snake lily | *Gladiolus oppositiflorus* | |
| | | *Gladiolus papilio* | |
| Araceae (arum lilies) | | *Tritonia disticha* | |
| *Zantedeschia albomaculata* | kleinvarkblom | *Tritonia lineata* | |
| *Zantedeschia pentlandii* | yellow arum | *Tritonia nelsonii* | |
| *Zantedeschia rehmannii* | persvarkblom | *Watsonia densiflora* | |

such as gloriosas and the deciduous agapanthus. The deciduous agapanthus species are particularly useful in mixed plantings with winter-growing species such as *Chasmanthe floribunda*.

### Planting

The rootstocks are planted out in spring at the same depths recommended for container subjects, but in sandy soil they can be planted deeper.

### Watering

A very good soaking once per week is recommended if natural precipitation is lacking during the summer-growing season.

Opposite: *Zantedeschia albomaculata* 'Helen O'Connor'

Below: *Cyrtanthus guthrieae*

Right: *Cyrtanthus obliquus*

# CULTIVATION OF EVERGREEN SPECIES

The evergreen species occur naturally in both the winter and summer rainfall areas, but a substantial number are to be found in areas of year-round rainfall, such as the southern Cape, and in the subtropical, coastal areas of KwaZulu-Natal and the Eastern Cape Province. This group also undergoes a short dormant period at some stage in the year while maintaining the older leaves. They generally produce additional new foliage in spring and summer. The very wide-ranging habits of evergreen species (from deep shade to full sun) make them invaluable to the gardener, both as container and garden subjects. They can be grown in most parts of South Africa, except in areas experiencing very cold winters. Several species of evergreen bulbous plants are perfectly hardy in mild parts of the Northern Hemisphere, such as in the southwest of England. These include *Dierama* species, the evergreen and deciduous *Agapanthus* species, *Moraea huttonii* and most *Kniphofia* species. Cold tender species require the protection of the cool greenhouse.

## Container subjects

### Aspect and growing medium

Most evergreen species suitable for containers require a partially shaded position (eg *Albuca nelsonii, Haemanthus albiflos* and *Tulbaghia simmleri*) while others need full sun (eg *Aristea spiralis*) or full shade (eg *Scadoxus membranaceus*). It is important to know the growth habits of the species in the wild in order to cultivate them successfully. Evergreen species in containers are very decorative when grouped together in large pots on a stoep (veranda) or balcony, and they generally prefer a rich, well-drained medium.

A 35 cm pot is the most convenient one in which to grow the larger species such as *Clivia miniata*, *Agapanthus comptonii* and

Above: *Kniphofia linearifolia*

Left: *Veltheimia bracteata*

Opposite left: *Clivia miniata* var. *citrina*

Opposite right: *Scadoxus multiflorus* subsp. *katharinae*

### Recommended evergreen species for containers

| Species | Common name |
|---|---|
| **Agapanthaceae** | |
| *Agapanthus comptonii* | |
| **Alliaceae** | |
| *Tulbaghia simmleri* | |
| *Tulbaghia violacea* | wildeknoflok |
| **Amaryllidaceae** | |
| *Clivia caulescens* | stem clivia |
| *Clivia gardenii* | Major Garden's clivia |
| *Clivia miniata* | bush lily |
| *Clivia nobilis* | bush lily |
| *Cyrtanthus brachyscyphus* | kleinrooipypie |
| *Cyrtanthus elatus* | George lily |
| *Cyrtanthus epiphyticus* | boomlelie |
| *Cyrtanthus eucallus* | |
| *Cyrtanthus guthrieae* | Bredasdorp lily |
| *Cyrtanthus herrei* | |
| *Cyrtanthus mackenii* | Ifafa lily |
| *Cyrtanthus montanus* | |
| *Cyrtanthus obliquus* | Knysna lily |
| *Cyrtanthus sanguineus* | Nahoon lily, Keilelie |
| *Haemanthus albiflos* | paint brush |
| *Nerine filamentosa* | |
| *Nerine filifolia* | |
| *Nerine masoniorum* | |
| *Nerine undulata* | |
| *Scadoxus membranaceus* | |
| **Hyacinthaceae** | |
| *Albuca nelsonii* | |
| *Ledebouria revoluta* | |
| *Veltheimia bracteata* | forest lily |
| **Iridaceae** | |
| *Gladiolus ochroleucus* | |

*Cyrtanthus herrei*, while 25 and 30 cm pots are suitable for the smaller *Cyrtanthus* and *Nerine* species. The smaller evergreen *Cyrtanthus* species are also grown to great advantage in 25 cm diameter hanging baskets (eg *C. sanguineus* and *C. montanus*).

**Recommended evergreen species for gardens**

| Species | Common name |
|---|---|
| Agapanthaceae | |
| *Agapanthus comptonii* | |
| *Agapanthus praecox* | bloulelie |
| Alliaceae | |
| *Tulbaghia simmleri* | |
| *Tulbaghia violacea* | wildeknoflok |
| Amaryllidaceae | |
| *Clivia caulescens* | stem clivia |
| *Clivia gardenii* | Major Garden's clivia |
| *Clivia miniata* | bush lily |
| *Clivia nobilis* | bush lily |
| *Cyrtanthus brachyscyphus* | kleinrooipypie |
| *Cyrtanthus elatus* | George lily |
| *Cyrtanthus mackenii* | Ifafa lily |
| *Haemanthus deformis* | |
| *Nerine filifolia* | |
| *Nerine masoniorum* | |
| *Scadoxus membranaceus* | |
| Asphodelaceae | |
| *Kniphofia baurii* | |
| *Kniphofia laxiflora* | torch lily |
| *Kniphofia linearifolia* | |
| *Kniphofia praecox* | |
| *Kniphofia rooperi* | |
| *Kniphofia uvaria* | red-hot poker |
| Haemodoraceae | |
| *Wachendorfia thyrsiflora* | rooikanol |
| Hyacinthaceae | |
| *Albuca nelsonii* | |
| *Veltheimia bracteata* | forest lily |
| Iridaceae | |
| *Aristea ecklonii* | |
| *Aristea major* | |
| *Dierama dracomontanum* | |
| *Dierama pendulum* | harebell |
| *Dierama pulcherrimum* | |
| *Dierama robustum* | |
| *Dietes bicolor* | |
| *Dietes butcheriana* | |
| *Dietes grandiflora* | |
| *Moraea huttonii* | |
| *Moraea spathulata* | |
| *Watsonia angusta* | rooikanolpypie |
| *Watsonia fourcadei* | |
| *Watsonia pillansii* | |
| *Watsonia tabularis* | |

### Planting and watering

Planting-up new pots of evergreen species can be done immediately after the flowering period, and generally they should remain undisturbed for several years. Certain evergreen *Cyrtanthus* species such as *C. montanus* and *C. herrei* require infrequent watering, but for most evergreen container subjects, a good soaking once a week throughout the year is recommended. Species with vigorous root systems like *Agapanthus comptonii* and *Tulbaghia violacea* need to be divided and re-potted every three years, when grown in containers.

Opposite: *Agapanthus comptonii* subsp. *longitubus*

## Garden subjects

### Aspect and growing medium

Evergreen species in the garden can remain in the same position for many years. Several prefer a full sun situation, such as *Dietes, Kniphofia* and *Watsonia* species, but others flourish in full or semi-shade (*Clivia miniata* and *Scadoxus membranaceus*). A number of sun-loving species such as *Agapanthus praecox* and *Dietes grandiflora* will also flourish in full shade, but will then flower infrequently, if at all. In general, a very rich, well-drained

growing medium containing well-rotted manure and compost is required for most species.

## Planting and watering

Planting out evergreen species in the garden after lifting and dividing is best done straight after the flowering period; new plantings should be kept constantly moist until established. If natural precipitation is lacking, a good soaking every one to two weeks is recommended for established plants throughout the year.

Above: *Haemanthus deformis*

Right: *Moraea barnardiella (Galaxia barnardii)*

Opposite: *Gladiolus stefaniae*

# PROPAGATION

Bulbous plants are propagated in order to increase numbers and maintain species in cultivation over a long period. The following methods are recommended.

**Seed**

In general, the winter-growing species are sown in autumn (March to May), and the summer-growing species in spring (August to October). Evergreen species from the winter rainfall areas are best sown in autumn and those from the summer rainfall areas in spring. Exceptions to the above general rules are the *Agapanthus* species and all members of the Amaryllidaceae, which should be sown as soon as they are ripe. Generally speaking, fresh seed of bulbous plants germinates very readily, but there are certain exceptions, such as *Sandersonia aurantiaca*, which can take up to three or four years to germinate.

Regarding *Sandersonia*, several germination-breaking techniques are practised by commercial growers in New Zealand (Finnie & van Staden, 1996). These include 'leaving the seeds in porous nets in a cold mountain stream for the winter and letting the ovaries degenerate into a "mush" over winter, and planting the resulting mush'. Finnie and van Staden also report that 'using one or a combination of increased oxygen tension, scarification, stratification, endosperm damage or lipid

Left: Successful germination of *Sandersonia aurantiaca* seeds after 14 months

Below left: *Zantedeschia rehmannii* seedlings in seed tray

Opposite: *Lachenalia purpureo-caerulea* leaf cuttings in rooting medium

Below: Young seedlings of winter-growing bulb species in raised bed

mobilization significantly increases germination of *Sandersonia* seeds'. Deep seed trays or pots should be used and the sowing medium should preferably be sterilized. The sowing medium used will depend on the species, but a good general medium is equal parts river- or industrial sand, and fine compost or loam. For the more delicate species, the amount of compost and loam should be reduced. Seed must be sown thinly to prevent

overcrowding and to allow sufficient room for the developing rootstocks. Seed of most species is covered with a thin layer of sand, while the large fleshy seeds of many of the amaryllid genera like *Clivia* and *Crinum* are simply pressed into the medium, to rest at or just below soil level. An exception is the genus *Cyrtanthus* whose flat dry seeds can also be germinated by placing in glass containers filled with water, which should be replaced about once a week. When the seedlings have produced a few leaves, they are then transferred to pots or seed trays. The seedlings of all bulbous plants should remain in the seed tray or pot for at least one full season. In many instances they should remain undisturbed for two to three seasons before being planted out into permanent containers or into the garden.

**Offsets, bulbils and cormels**

Offsets formed on bulbs and corms are removed during the dormant period, when large enough. Corm offsets can be stored dry until the following planting time, but bulb offsets of species with perennial fleshy roots, eg members of the Amaryllidaceae, should be replanted immediately. Several species of *Lachenalia* reproduce by bulbil formation on leaf bases or at the tips of stolons, and similarly, numerous members of the Iridaceae also produce cormels at the tips of stolons. Bulbils and cormels should be removed during the dormant period and stored until planting time.

**Division of rhizomatous rootstocks**

Those genera with rhizomatous rootstocks, such as *Agapanthus* and *Kniphofia*, are propagated vegetatively by lifting a large clump and prizing it apart with two large forks placed back to back in the centre. The foliage is then cut back by about one third, and the roots by about two thirds, and the individual portions of rootstock are re-planted as soon as possible. *Clivia*

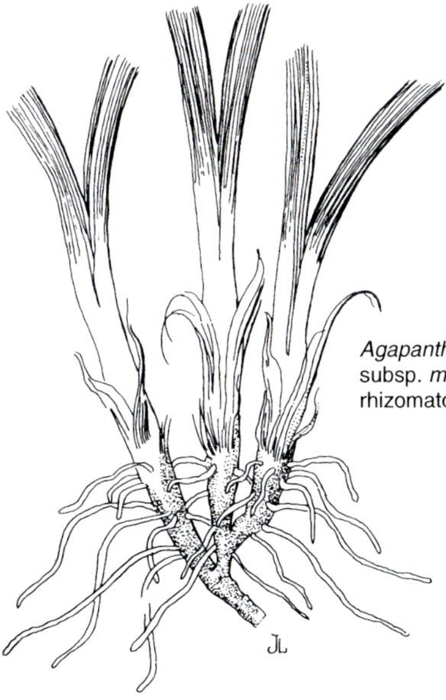


*Agapanthus praecox* subsp. *minimus* – rhizomatous rootstock

clumps are divided in the same way except that the leaves and roots should not be cut back at all.

**Leaf cuttings**

Propagation by leaf cuttings is an effective way of increasing stocks of the genus *Lachenalia*. Leaves for cutting material should be virus-free (see Pests and diseases on page 51) and preferably in active growth. Depending on leaf size, the leaf material is cut into cross sections and placed in a well-drained rooting medium such as equal parts river-sand and vermiculite, with the base of the cutting about 1 cm below the surface. The cuttings are placed in a shaded position and kept only slightly moist. Bulblets begin to form at the base of the cutting after about one month and they should be removed and stored at the end of the growing season and planted out in autumn.

# CARE OF PLANTS

## Feeding

Indigenous bulbous plants can, in general, be grown successfully without any supplementary feeding because of their low nutritional requirements, but this is not to say that feeding is not recommended. On the contrary, most species respond very readily to fertilizers with a high potassium but low nitrogen content. Slow-release fertilizers like Osmocote can be incorporated into the upper part of the growing medium, or sprinkled on the surface. Liquid fertilizers, such as Kelpak 66, can be used at a weaker rate than recommended, at fortnightly intervals. Gross feeders like *Agapanthus* and *Clivia* benefit greatly from applications of granular fertilizer like 3:1:5 applied during the summer growing period. Additional trace nutrient element fertilizer such as Trelmix is especially recommended for clivias if plants show deficiencies.

## Pests and diseases

Under cultivation, bulbous plants are subject to various pests and diseases: the more important ones are listed with

Above: *Babiana blanda*

Left: B*abiana villosa*

Opposite: Bulblet formation on leaf cutting of *Lachenalia purpureo-caerulea*

suggested methods and measures for their control, both environmentally friendly and chemical.

**Environmentally friendly treatments**

Pest or disease

Aphid (green fly) These small green or black sucking insects are usually found on developing flower buds and on the foliage of irids like *Gladiolus* and *Moraea*. Aphids are transmitters of viral diseases.

Make up a solution of 5 ml liquid soap in 1 *l* water. Spray the aphids away with the solution. Ladybirds are natural predators of aphids.

Lily borer (Amaryllis caterpillar) These highly destructive black and yellow striped caterpillars bore into the leaves of summer-growing amaryllids, eventually entering the bulb.

Remove the caterpillars by hand, or cut away and squash affected foliage.

Mealy bug These oval-shaped sucking insects have a white waxy covering, and are found in large numbers between bulb scales and corm tunics as well as at the base of leaves. They secrete honeydew, are spread by ants, and are the transmitters of viral diseases.

Remove insects by hand or squash them against the bulb or corm. Mix equal parts methylated spirits and water and remove any remaining mealy bugs by dipping a cotton wool bud into the solution and wiping insects away.

Red spider mite These tiny red, spider-like mites attack the foliage of many irids like *Gladiolus* and *Babiana*, and amaryllids like *Cyrtanthus*, to a lesser extent. They give the foliage a silvery-bronze sheen and multiply extremely rapidly. They are usually found on the undersides of the leaves.

Soak 20 cigarette stubs in 1 *l* water for one week. Add 2.5 ml liquid soap and spray the insects off the leaves.

Slugs and snails are active at night and cause damage to the leaves of amaryllids like *Crinum* and *Brunsvigia*, and attack buds and leaves of a wide range of smaller bulbous plants. They are transmitters of viral diseases.

Apply tobacco dust in a circle around the base of and at a short distance away from the plants, or sprinkle a few grains of salt directly onto active slugs and snails. Snails can also be removed by hand and

Snout beetle feeding on flowers of *Dietes grandiflora*

Opposite: Lily borer (amaryllis caterpillar) devastates all amaryllids

squashed, and slugs can be picked up with tweezers. Alternatively, keep ducks to do the job for you (Dutch quackers or Muscovies are ideal). Bantam poultry such as Silkies and Pekins cause minimal damage and are beneficial in ridding the garden of many pests like caterpillars, beetles and small snails, as well as fertilizing the soil with their droppings.

**Damping-off** Seedlings are attacked at the base of the young plant, mainly by the *Pythium* fungus, causing the plant to collapse.

Jeyes Fluid can be used to drench the soil before sowing. Mix 75 ml in 10 *l* of water for each square metre of seedling soil. Sprinkle the solution on the soil and cover with a plastic sheet for 10 days before sowing. Seed should always be sown sparsely so that seedlings are well ventilated and the leaves can dry off quickly after watering.

**Viral infection** Viral organisms are transmitted in the sap of an infected plant to a healthy plant by transmitting agents such as aphids, mealy bugs and snails, and on cutting instruments like secateurs. Viruses cause a variety of symptoms such as deformed leaves and discolouration patterns on leaves and flowers in the form of mosaics, mottling or light-coloured streaks. Lachenalias, ornithogalums and brunsvigias are particularly prone to viral infections.

A plant displaying viral symptoms should be isolated as soon as possible, treated against mites and given a balanced fertilizer which includes trace nutrient elements. If the symptoms persist, the plant should be destroyed, preferably by burning.

**Snout beetle** These small grey beetles are active in summer, and chew away at the leaves of summer-growing and evergreen

amaryllids in particular, and other summer-growing bulbs like *Galtonia*, to a lesser extent. The beetles are only active at night.The beetles hide on the undersides of leaf bases during the day. Remove them by hand and crush them.

### Chemical treatments

Pest or disease

(See more comprehensive description of pests or diseases under 'Environmentally friendly treatments' on page 52)

Aphid (green fly)

Chlorpyrifos (eg Chlorpirifos) as a full cover spray: 10 ml/10 *l* water.

Mercaptothion (eg Malathion) as a full cover spray: 25 ml/10 *l* water.

Lily borer (Amaryllis caterpillar)

Carbaryl (eg Carbaryl) as a full cover spray: 15 g/10 *l* water.

**Mealy bug**
Chlorpyrifos (eg Chlorpirifos) as a drench or full cover spray: 10 ml/10*l* water.
Mercaptothion (eg Malathion) as a full cover spray: 25ml/10*l* water.
**Red spider mite**
Oleum (eg Oleum) as a full cover spray: 200ml/10*l* water.
Chlorpyrifos (eg Chlorpirifos) as a full cover spray: 10ml/10*l* water.
**Slugs and snails**
Metaldehyde (eg Snailbait) as a bait.
Methiocarb (eg Mesurol) as a bait.
**Thrips** Minute, narrow sucking insects most often found attacking the flower buds and foliage of summer-growing gladioli, leaving characteristic white streaks. They are transmitters of viral diseases.
Mercaptothion (eg Malathion) as a full cover spray: 25ml/10*l* water.
Tenthion (eg Lebaycid) as a full cover spray: 10ml/10*l* water.
Chlorpyrifos (eg Chlorpirifos) as a full cover spray: 10ml/10*l* water.
**Whitefly** Small white insects mainly active in summer, sucking the sap from the undersides of leaves, especially on summer-growing arums (*Zantedeschia*).
Phenothrin (eg Garden Gun) as a full cover aerosol spray.
Diazinon (eg Dazzel) as a full cover spray: 12ml/10*l* water.

Opposite: *Ixia viridiflora*

Ornamental Pekin Bantams rid the garden of many pests, and fertilize the soil. Do not use chemical treatments when keeping free-range poultry.

**Snout beetle**
Cypermethrin (eg Ripcord) as a full cover spray: 1 ml/10*l* water.
**Damping-off fungus**
Captab (eg Kaptan) as a soil drench: 20 g/10*l* water.
Pre-sowing treatment: Sterilize sowing medium or dust seeds with captab (eg Kaptan).
**Fungal rot** is noticed when leaves are slow to develop, appear unhealthy, or the growing shoot may fail to appear at all.

Lift and clean the rootstock, then cut away all infected parts and dust the whole rootstock with captab (eg Kaptan). Replant the rootstock in sterilized river-sand and place in a cool, shaded spot. If the plant recovers, bring it out into the open again.
**Rust** is recognized as reddish-brown pustules on leaves, which break open and liberate powder-like spores. Dieramas and gladioli are very susceptible.
Mancozeb (eg Dithane) as a full cover spray: 20 g/10*l* water.
**Leaf spots** are caused by various fungi, especially during wet weather. The disease is first noticed as brown spots on leaves. These spots enlarge, resulting in a grey fungal growth.
Iprodione (eg Rovral) as a full cover spray: 200 ml/10*l* water

**The above mentioned chemicals are poisonous and potentially dangerous. They are to be applied with great care, only if absolutely necessary**

*Moraea aristata*

# FURTHER READING


Barnhoorn, F. 1995. *Growing Bulbs in Southern Africa*. Southern Book Publishers, Halfway House.

Bryan, J.E. 1989. *Bulbs*. Vol. 1 and 2. Timber Press, Oregon.

Dahlgren, R.M.T., H.T. Clifford and P.F. Yeo, 1985. *The Families of the Monocotyledons*. Springer-Verlag, Heidelberg.

Doutt, R.L. 1994. *Cape Bulbs*. Timber Press, Oregon.

Duncan, G.D. 1982a. Ten *Babiana* species for promotion . *Veld & Flora* 68(2): 47-48.

Duncan, G.D. 1982b. *Gladiolus ochroleucus* – a desirable species for pot culture. *Veld & Flora* 68(4): 112-113.

Duncan, G.D. 1985. Notes on the genus *Clivia* Lindl. with particular reference to *C. miniata Regel* var. *citrina* Watson. *Veld & Flora* 71(3): 84-85.

Duncan, G.D. 1985. *Agapanthus* species – their potential, and the introduction of ten selected forms. *Veld & Flora* 71(4): 122-125.

Duncan, G.D. 1988. The *Lachenalia* Handbook. *Annals of Kirstenbosch Botanic Gardens*. 17. National Botanical Institute, Cape Town.

Duncan, G.D. 1990. *Cyrtanthus* – its horticultural potential, Part 1. *Veld & Flora* 76(1): 18-21.

Duncan, G.D. 1990. *Cyrtanthus* – its horticultural potential, Part 2. *Veld & Flora* 76(2): 54-56.

Duncan, G.D. 1990. *Cyrtanthus* – its horticultural potential, Part 3. *Veld & Flora* 76(3): 72-73.

Duncan, G.D. 1991. Clivias and their cultivation. *Parks and Grounds* 59: 21-22.

Duncan, G.D. 1993. Wild irises for the garden *Veld & Flora* 79(3): 74-76.

Duncan, G.D. 1996. *Growing South African bulbous plants*. National Botanical Institute, Cape Town.

Duncan, G.D. 1997. Moraeas of the Western Cape. *Veld & Flora* 83(2): 42-44.

Duncan, G.D. 1998. The Kay Bergh Bulb House *Veld & Flora* 84(3): 80-81.

Duncan, G.D. 1998. *Grow Agapanthus*. (Kirstenbosch Gardening Series). National Botanical Institute, Cape Town.

Duncan, G.D. 1998. Notes on the genus *Lachenalia*. *Herbertia* 53: 40-48.

Duncan, G.D. 1999. *Grow Clivias*. (Kirstenbosch Gardening Series). National Botanical Institute, Cape Town.

Duncan, G.D. 1999. Ixias for pot and garden. *Veld & Flora* 85(2): 78-79.

Du Plessis, N.M. and G.D. Duncan, 1989. *Bulbous plants of southern Africa*. Tafelberg, Cape Town.

Dyer, R.A. 1976. *The genera of the Southern African Flowering Plants*. Vol. 2: *Gymnosperms and Monocotyledons*. Botanical Research Institute, Pretoria.

Eliovson, S. 1967. *Bulbs for the gardener*. Howard Timmins, Cape Town.
Finnie, J.F. and J. van Staden, 1996. *Sandersonia aurantiaca* Hook. (Christmas Bells): Micropropagation and *in vitro* production of Colchicine. *Biotechnology in Agriculture and Forestry* 37: 355-369.
Grey, C.H. 1937. *Hardy Bulbs*. Vol.1: *Iridaceae*. Williams & Northgate, London.
Grey, C.H. 1938. *Hardy Bulbs*. Vol.2: *Amaryllidaceae, Commelinaceae, Haemodoraceae, Orchidaceae, Scitamineae*. Williams & Northgate, London.
Grey, C.H. 1938. *Hardy Bulbs*. Vol.3: *Liliaceae*. Williams & Northgate, London.
Hartmann, H.T. and D.E. Kester, 1975. *Plant Propagation – Principles and Practices*. Prentice-Hall, Englewood Cliffs, New Jersey.
Hobbs, J. and T. Hatch, 1994. *Best Bulbs for Temperate Climates*. Timber Press, Oregon.
Jeppe, B.J. 1989. *Spring and Winter Flowering Bulbs of the Cape*. Oxford University Press, Cape Town.
Manning, J. and P. Goldblatt, 1996. *West Coast*. (South African Wildflower Guide 7). Botanical Society and Darling Wildflower Society.

Mathew, B. 1987. *Flowering Bulbs for the Garden* (Kew Gardening Guide). Collingridge Books, in association with the Royal Botanic Garden, Kew.
Oliver, I.B. 1993. *Growing South African succulents*. National Botanical Institute, Cape Town.
Oliver, I.B. 1998. *Grow Succulents*. (Kirstenbosch Gardening Series) National Botanical Institute, Cape Town.
Phillips, R. and M. Rix, 1989. *Bulbs*. Pan Books, London.
Rix, M, 1983. *Growing Bulbs*. Croom Helm, London & Canberra.
Rix, M. and R. Phillips, 1981. *The Bulb Book*. Pan Books, London.
Smith, C.A. 1966. *Common Names of South African Plants*. Department of Agricultural Technical Services, Pretoria.
Wager, V.A. 1984. *Plant Pests and Diseases*. Johnathan Ball Publishers, Johannesburg.

Left: *Dierama pendulum*

Below: *Ornithogalum dubium* (orange form)

Opposite: *Haemanthus coccineus*

# USEFUL ADDRESSES

**Botanical Society of South Africa**

By joining the Botanical Society of South Africa, one can take advantage of its annual catalogue of surplus seed supplied by the National Botanical Institute. Usually included is a wide selection of bulbous species. At the Society's Annual Garden Fair at Kirstenbosch, one can purchase bulbs of a number of species. The Society's quarterly journal *Veld & Flora* lists several specialist bulb nurseries in its classified advertisements, and carries the occasional article on bulbous plants.

Further information on the Botanical Society can be obtained from:

The Botanical Society of South Africa
Private Bag X10 Newlands
7725
South Africa
Tel: +27 021 797 2090
Fax: +27 021 797 2376
E-mail: botsocsa@gem.co.za

**Indigenous Bulb Association of South Africa**

Membership of the Indigenous Bulb Association of South Africa (IBSA) will keep you in touch with others interested in bulbs. The Association publishes an annual bulletin and holds meetings, outings and talks. IBSA distributes a big variety of seed of bulbous plants and bulbs/corms, but only to members. Membership is open to any and every bulb enthusiast. Its aim is conservation through cultivation, and members grow a wide range of rare species.

Further information on IBSA can be obtained from:
The Secretary
IBSA
P.O. Box 12265
N1 City
7463
South Africa
Tel: +27 021 558 1690
Fax: +27 021 558 1690

### Clivia Club

Membership of the Clivia Club will keep you in touch with other Clivia enthusiasts, whether they be keen amateurs, specialist growers or professional researchers. The Club publishes a quaterly newsletter, holds meetings, arranges flower shows and supplies seeds and plants.

Those wishing to join the Clivia Club and who reside in South Africa are encouraged to contact their local Clivia Club Branch in either the Northern Branch, the KwaZulu-Natal Branch or the Cape Province Branch. Those residing in provinces without a local branch should contact the Head Office. Those residing in Australia should contact the Australian Branch, while those residing in all other countries should contact the Head Office, South Africa.

#### South Africa

The Secretary
Clivia Club (Head Office)
Private Bag X7
Claremont
7735
Tel: +27 021 762 1166
Fax: +27 021 797 0002
E-mail: woodward@nbict.nbi.ac.za

The Chairman
Clivia Club (Northern Branch)
P.O. Box 99583
Garsfontein
0042
Tel: +27 012 998 5942
E-mail: vlok@alpha.unisa.ac.za

The Chairman
Clivia Club (KwaZulu-Natal Branch)
P.O. Box 74
Eston
3740
Tel/Fax: +27 031 258 1978

The Chairman
Clivia Club (Cape Province Branch)
Private Bag X7
Claremont
7735
Tel: +27 021 762 1166
Fax: +27 021 797 0002
E-mail: woodward@nbict.nbi.ac.za

#### Australia

The Chairman
Clivia Club (Australian Branch)
593 Hawkesbury Road
Winmalee
New South Wales 2777
Tel: +61 4754 3287
E-mail: cliviasmith@hotmail.com

### South African Arum Club

This newly formed Club provides information about all South African *Zantedeschia* species (arums). Members receive a free arum, newsletters and advice.

Further information can be obtained from:
South African Arum Club
P.O. Box 1552
Kempton Park
1620
South Africa
Tel: +27 011 082 887 6602
Fax: +27 011 744 1313

*Crocosmia aurea*

# SOURCES OF SUPPLY

**South Africa**

The Croft Wild Bulb Nursery
P.O. Box 61
4930 Stutterheim
Tel/Fax: +27 043 683 2796

Cape Flora Nursery
P.O. Box 10556
6015 Linton Grange
Tel: +27 041 732 096
Fax: +27 041 733 188

Cape Seed and Bulb Nursery
P.O. Box 6363
7612 Uniedal
Tel: +27 021 8879 418
Fax: +27 021 8870 823

Kirstenbosch Garden Centre
Private Bag X01
7725 Newlands
Tel: +27 021 762 1621
Fax: +27 021 762 0923

New Plant Nursery
P.O. Box 4138
6539 George East
Tel: +27 044 8711 806
Fax: +27 044 8712 732

Penrock Seeds
P.O. Box 571
2037 Highlands North
Fax: +27 011 887 4158

Random Harvest Nursery
P.O. Box 4216
2040 Honeydew
Fax: +27 011 957 2399

Rust-en-Vrede Nursery
P.O. Box 753
7561 Brackenfell
Tel: +27 021 981 4515
Fax: +27 021 981 0050

Shosholoza Nursery
P.O. Box 63
3300 Mooi River

Silverhill Seeds
P.O. Box 53108
7745 Kenilworth
Tel: +27 021 762 4245
Fax: +27 021 797 6609

Summerfield's Indigenous Bulbs and Seed
P.O. Box 5150
7135 Helderberg
Tel/Fax: +27 021 855 2442

Witkoppen Wild Flower Nursery
P.O. Box 67036
2021 Bryanston
Tel: +27 011 465 7793
Fax: +27 011 465 7792

# INDEX

Page numbers in bold denote illustrations.

*Gladiolus priorii*